GW00470678

Astrology

A Beginner's Guide to Understanding the 12 Zodiac Signs and Their Secret Meanings

Free membership into the Mastermind Self Development Group!

For a limited time, you can join the Mastermind Self Development Group for free! You will receive videos and articles from top authorities in self-development as well as a special group only offers on new books and training programs. There will also be a monthly member only draw that gives you a chance to win any book from your Kindle wish list!

If you sign up through this link: http://www.mastermindselfdevelopment.com/specialreport you will also get a special free report on the Wheel of Life. This report will give you a visual look at your current life and then take you through a series of exercises that will help you plan what your perfect life looks like. The workbook does not end there; we then take you through a process to help you plan how to achieve that perfect life. The process is very powerful and has the potential to change your life forever. Join the group now and start to change your life! http://www.mastermindselfdevelopment.com/specialreport

MASTERMIND
Self Development

Table of Contents

Introduction

I want to thank you and congratulate you for downloading *Astrology: A Beginner's Guide to Understanding the 12 Zodiac Signs and Their Secret Meanings*.

What can we know about someone upon first meeting them? We can see their style of dress, their mannerisms, and start to draw some conclusions to ourselves. Maybe we can imagine what type of music that person enjoys, or perhaps make a prediction as to what they do for a living. These are small details that we are merely guessing based on first appearances. Even if we are correct in our initial assumptions about someone, our initial impressions have little to do with the core personality of the person we are meeting. We know nothing of their strengths and weaknesses, their passions, their wit, their sense of humor and so much more.

For centuries, our ancestors have used the signs of the zodiac to gain insight into others. Some view this as mysticism, but I believe that the breakdown of personalities, their passions and interests, can be used to better understand our fellow man. There are so many views that we disagree with, but if we could just understand the perspective of our neighbors, perhaps we would find that we have more in common than we think.

With just a date of birth, we can discover the personalities of the people around us. We can gain insight into whether they are analytical or emotional, their family values, even their drive for success. What would you do with this information if you could be privy to such secretes upon first meeting someone? It truly allows us to gain insight into another person, insight that was previously blocked by months of conversation in which you get to know someone. The goal of this book is to teach you the basics of the astrological signs, their character traits, strengths and weaknesses. How you decide to use this information is up to you, but I hope that is serves the purpose of promoting better understanding of your friends, family, and even those that you disagree with.

There is practicality in the study of astrology. You can use the insight studying the signs of the zodiac offers to your advantage and surround yourself with positive thinkers, or people with the same drive for success that you do. In terms of love, you can identify the type of characteristics that you want in your ideal mate and match them through the signs of the zodiac. This is the magic that astrology offers; a fascinating look at the base archetype personalities and how they manifest in the many people in our daily lives. By studying the astrological sign of a person, you can better understand the relationship that you have, revealing truths for why conflict has arisen in the past, and explaining why you agree on certain topics but are so vehemently conflicted on others.

Whether merely a curiosity, or if you are actively seeking to invoke the knowledge of the signs of the zodiac in your everyday life, this book offers the key information that you need to truly understand the twelve signs of the zodiac and the secrets that lie within. Continue reading and soon the secrets of the signs of the zodiac will be revealed to you.

Alex

Chapter 1: Aries

March 21st – April 19th

Aries is the first of the zodiac signs, and accordingly is best described as competitive, head strong, and a constant desire to be in the lead. I have known many Aries in my life, but my fondest recollection comes from high school, when I befriended one of the best athletes in our school. All zodiac signs have strengths and weaknesses, but to add context to these traits, I want to use real life examples whenever possible. If you think back on your own life, with each description you will find that there is certainly a character from your past that aligns with many values of their zodiac sign. For Aries, these characteristics are best exemplified through my high school athlete friend, a strong, tough and rambunctious individual that needed to be first in anything that was a contest.

Aries tend to be of average to slightly above average intellect, but don't let this have you believe that they cannot be the head of major organizations. What they might lack in intellect in comparison to other signs, they more than makeup for in their drive and passion for success. A key way to engage with an Aries is to treat all activities like a contest, provided you are fine with not winning every time. Competition is the first key characteristic of an Aries. An Aries needs a sense of competition to get engaged, and it is perhaps their greatest strength and weakness. Even when an Aries isn't particularly interested in a topic or activity, they will become motivated to learn and understand the task at hand if it is made a competition. This perfectly describes my friend in high school. He was into athletics far more than schoolwork, but whenever the classroom decided to turn learning into a competitive game, he would soar to the occasion. For example, our math teacher once divided the room into two groups and had each half of the classroom answer questions against each other. Our teacher turned our most recent algebra lesson into a game, and suddenly my friend that had maybe a passing interest in algebra at the most, immediately became engaged. I saw him work harder in that single class period than perhaps at any time in the semester. This is the mindset of an Aries, and as long as everything is framed as a form of competition, an Aries is likely to find great success. My friend in this instance demonstrated more of his knowledge of algebra than he had on any test handed out by our teacher. Had my teacher framed more classes with this completive spirit, it would have done wonders for my friend and any other Aries in the classroom.

The competitive side of an Aries can easily be their greatest weaknesses as well. While it is fantastic that an Aries can rise to the occasion and get involved in any activity when it is treated as a competition, it is a competition that an Aries feels they *need* to win. They often tie their self worth into the actual winning of the game. This can lead to one of the most tragic combinations, an Aries that consistently loses. You may be familiar with type of personality, but this is someone that has a competitive edge to them but is saddened, has low self-esteem and is a sore loser. An Aries that succeeds in competition reinforces their ego and they can be fantastic people, but an Aries that has an inclination to lose in competition is doomed to think about their failures. This is the cruel fate that is bestowed upon some Aries. Competition is by and far the strongest trait that this sign exhibits, but there is more to an Aries than just competition to improve themselves; they also care deeply about other people.

The second defining trait of an Aries is that they are courageous. This often manifests in an Aries being a caring friend that is willing to put anything on the line to help out their friends. An Aries is responsible for their family, and they will be able to tough it through any situation if they believe that they are doing well for someone that they care about. This personality trait reveals itself in a 'get it done spirit' that can be quite practical in practice. This is the type of person that will have the drive to learn a trade and provide for their family if the situation calls for it. This is how that level of bravery brings itself to the surface in our modern society – someone that cares and has the due diligence to provide for his or her family.

The third defining trait of an Aries is their complete inability to be without activity. This is partially a result of their desire for competition, but an Aries also does not like to be alone with their thoughts. They hate the idea of being passive and will be proactive no matter the setting. I like to picture this as the new found homeowner, and the Aries that cannot sit still for a single weekend until every fix and maintenance job on the house is completed. There is no such thing as downtime for an Aries, and as long as they have a productive task that needs doing, they will be willing to give it a head start and get to work.

If you know an Aries in your life, it is my suggestion that you tap into their strength and desire to accomplish and finish tasks. This is a great friend to go to the gym with – not only will they keep you motivated when you are actually working out, but they will also put the fire under you to ensure that you go consistently. Other signs can tap into the strength of an Aries in this way; they simply must engage themselves in the activities of an Aries and some of that competitive spirit and drive to accomplish the task at hand will rub off. This is a great personality to engage on this level, and an Aries is also a friend that you can count on. They will always rise to the occasion, and are deeply dependable. They will always be there for you and it would be wise to incorporate a close tied Aries in your life.

Chapter 2: Taurus

April 20th – May 20th

A Taurus is the steady engine of the zodiac signs. They require maintenance through friendships and lavish materials around them, but in exchange they offer one of the most consistent moods and a desire to finish the task at hand. A Taurus is more attached to their routine than any other sign. They cannot, for example, be on a rotating schedule at work. They need to have the same hours, and are at their best when they are focusing on the same tasks over and over again. A great fit for employment for a Taurus is someone that works in accounting, or a field where it requires using a similar tactic to solve each and every problem. A poor line of work for a Taurus would be a waiter; the rapid change in tasks and the inconsistency in a restaurant setting is a recipe for disaster with a Taurus. In fact, their stubbornness often ensures that they are not suited to customer relation roles at all. Like most zodiac signs, their greatest strength in this regard, consistency, also proves to be the source of many of their personality weaknesses, like stubbornness.

My wife is a Taurus; she is the most stable person in my life. Without the aid of alarm clock, she is up at the same time each and every day. She has a routine so firm that you would think she had an endless set of timers to help her keep to her rigid schedule, but this is just her personality. She has something imbedded in her that just forces her from one activity to the next. Whereas I might forget to do a chore around the house, she cannot rest until everything that needs to be done is completed. This is a result of the drive of the Taurus and their desire to be a dependency to all other signs. They feel that their worth is defined by their consistency, both to themselves and to others. Provided they are in a setting where they are able to carry out the same routine, a Taurus can be extremely powerful in this regard.

This desire for routine and a hatred for a break from it is also a great point of many of their character flaws. A Taurus is one of the most stubborn signs, and when they are confronted with a reality they do not like, and especially a task they do not want to partake in, they can be anything but amenable. They will get so deep into their own corner of thought that it is almost not worth arguing with a Taurus. This might sound like one of the most damning character flaws, but with it also comes their uncompromising nature. Their stubbornness in routine and actions is true through their ideals and worldview. They will not budge on the morals that they have adopted due to this stubbornness, and this is something to be cherished.

A Taurus has a desire for fine materials and likes to envelop themselves in comfortable fabrics. They hate synthetic materials and would rather wear a cotton sweater in the rain than have to deal with the irritation of a synthetic jacket. I like to think of this aspect of a Taurus, their desire for fine fabrics, as a sort of maintenance cost of their personality. For the consistency that is received from a Taurus, something that can be of use to less reliable signs, they need to feel comfortable, and they need the aid of fabric to do this. This is often construed as a Taurus having a desire to shop frequently, especially for clothing, but this is only partially true. A Taurus does indeed shop for fabric and clothing quite frequently, but what they are seeking is not necessarily lavish designs, patterns or fashion, but rather the quality of the materials. For a Taurus, the build quality and the type of fabric for clothing is far more important than anything related to the style. I used this information to make a better decision on what gift to give my wife for her birthday. One of the things I got her was a blanket, made from 100% cotton. I got her other, more expensive gifts, but this is the one that will see the most use out of my wife. With soft fabrics and materials a Taurus can feel secure when their self esteem might waver – it simply allows for the consistently in their actions that is so central to a Taurus

It must be mentioned that a Taurus has a fine appreciation for the arts. They care a lot about music, painting and performance art. In addition, they like to work with their hands and at a consistent pace that they can set themselves. You will therefore find many Taurus like to knit, sew, or constantly have their hands occupied with a forward moving task. In fact, for the purpose of getting the attention of a Taurus consistently, you may want to put something in their hands that they can simply play with, as this will allow them to give you greater attention.

If you know a Taurus in your life, use their strength as being a consistent member of the family or of your office. In the office place, I think a Taurus can be immensely useful. As long as you understand that certain arguments will get nowhere because they can be stubborn, you can put to use their great strengths. A Taurus is unlikely to be late for work, and their drive for consistency in pace and execution in tasks make them unparalleled in ability for certain lines of work. You can use their strengths to run a more stable office – they will be the consistent employee that is always the same in terms of their desire to work, but also a stable member emotionally. They can tie an office place together, and give a signal to other workers to stay on task. This is not done out of pressure to perform because a Taurus is working, but rather because seeing a Taurus do their diligent work promotes others to do the same through their strong lead in getting things done.

Chapter 3: Gemini

May 21st-June 20th

My birthday falls under the sign of the Gemini. Gemini share an interesting sign because they have some remarkable strengths, but for those to be really brought to the limelight, they need the strength of another sign that can instill in them the self-esteem that they so often lack. A Gemini in many ways is the opposite of a Taurus, as they are not at all consistent. This inconsistency is true in every sense of the word; from their ability to work to their emotions about others and themselves, nothing is permanent for a Gemini, and this is their greatest weakness. Without a strong sign around them, someone to provide consistency and diligence, or at least an emotional outlet for a Gemini, a Gemini can become closeted off from the rest of the world. A Gemini, if they have the strength of another sign, has some remarkable strengths however, and their sense of curiosity is almost unrivaled among other signs.

A Gemini is best defined by their inconsistency, but even this inconsistently tends to fall between two different like archetypes. They are either to themselves, secluded or in a state of self-despair, or they are happy, wanting to spend as much time around other people as possible and are infinitely curious about the world. When a Gemini has the support that they require, they can do great work both artistically and practically. They are great problem solvers and are fantastic at thinking outside the box. They are excellent communicators and are able to get their point across clearly to other signs. Moreover, they are excellent negotiators as their ability to understand the ideas of others through communication allows them to put themselves in the shoes of another. These are their primary strengths, but this can provide for some remarkable results.

I already mentioned that I am a Gemini, and while I am trying to illustrate each sign with one person from my own life that exhibited these characteristics, for the purpose of this sign, I cannot talk about myself. I must defer to my brother, also born under the sign of the Gemini. He so perfectly exhibits the traits of a Gemini because of his strong sense of duality. He is very much either at the top of the world, or at the bottom of it. This is a common way in which their traits blend together. They have great ability to solve problems and to be a productive member in an office place, but their inability to deal with their own emotions manifests in a strong cynicism. They need a strong sign to support them, as without aid they often live a life of highs and lows. It is this inconsistently that a Gemini is not able to get away from unless a stronger sign in present, and for my brother this is true in his line of work. He does a type of solar panel construction for non-traditional homes. This is a line of work that requires lots of problem solving skills, and so it is perfect for my brother as a Gemini. The problem is that since this is a line of work where he is very much self employed, his ability to stay in business is entirely dependent on his ability to be consistent. If perhaps, he had a Scorpio, Aries or Taurus as a business partner, he would be better suited to the task. As it stands, he is someone that is capable of some truly amazing things, but his lack of consistency has hindered him every step of the way.

There are some other aspects to a Gemini that are worth noting, mainly their strong cynicism and adaptable nature. I don't believe that the cynicism of a Gemini is inherently a negative trait, although I can often understand if it is perceived as such. This type of cynicism though is helpful for humor, and so you will find that many Gemini in your life are small time comedians, enjoying the thrill of making their friends laugh. This serves more than just the friends of the Gemini though, as this type of humor allows a Gemini to feel like they are around family, and others that they can trust. They get this sense from others due to their humor – it is not a replacement for a long term partner, but in the immediate it can instill many of the feelings that a Gemini needs to feel good about themselves.

Their adaptable nature is also important. They have a strong duality that alternates between a strong ego and self-depreciation. They are accustomed to being on top of the world, as well as the being at the bottom of it, and these large swings are imbedded into the way that a Gemini thinks about the world. They do not believe anything to be truly permanent, and they are able to get used to any number of life styles, habits and routines. In fact, a Gemini is at their best when they do not have the same routine day in and day out. They need the ability to change their lifestyle on a whim, as this instills a form of self worth to them. They are so able to get used to new situations that they have a longing for change, as it makes them better understand the world than the rigid structure that they often have to force themselves into.

If you have a Gemini in your life, make the most of their humor and their curious nature. They are great people to go on trips with, or to merely exchange ideas and talk to. They tend to not be stubborn to new viewpoints, and can be very accommodating of any type of social circle. They frequently like to get out of their comfort zone and try new experiences, and so if you have a Gemini in your life, try and have them take you with them – they offer a view of the world that you simply cannot get from other signs.

Chapter 4: Cancer

June 21st – July 22nd

      Think back to elementary school. Picture your favorite teacher from this time, the one that loved and cared about his or her students. Think to the instructor that wanted to teach but knew how to have fun doing it. Other teachers may have feigned interest in their students, but with this one, you were sure that they were genuine. This person that you are imagining fits so many of the qualities of a Cancer, that they just might in fact be one. A Cancer cares about their family above all else. They are extremely loyal to their friends and family, and will do anything for a loved one in need. This matches well with their strengths as being understanding and compassionate of others, as well as being fiercely intelligent. They make great teachers, as they are people that both understand the material on hand and also have a great appreciation for their students.

      In my own experiences, when I think back to elementary school I am reminded of my first grade teacher, Ms. S. My first grade elementary school teacher was one of the tender's people I have ever met. It took me many years before I could look back on our experiences together through the lens of an adult. As a child I just thought of her as a sweet lady that truly loved to teach. Today, I see her as more than that. The fact that she was able to deal with thirty rambunctious kids is quite extraordinary. We never gave her an easy time, as no group of eight-year-old kids ever would do for a young woman, but she managed to handle us all with such ease. This exemplifies the strengths of a Cancer so well. She had these Cancer ideals flowing through her blood, and was able to persuade her entire class of little kids that learning truly was fun. This looks at just some of the major strengths of a Cancer; they are sympathetic, persuasive, emotional, loyal and extremely creative.

      She embodied many of these ideas, but by and far the most notable trait looking back on my experiences was just how persuasive she could be. How do you convince a classroom of thirty kids running around that they should all quiet down and open their books? The answer for another teacher might be to raise their voice, or maybe to send a child the most disruptive child to the principal's office, but not Mrs. S.; her strategy involved speaking to the children, and gaining the trust of the kids that could quiet down the entire classroom. She must have realized that if she could just connect with a few kids, and get them to cooperate, then the rest of the class would soon fall into line. To her credit, she was absolutely correct. She was able to convince the entire class by just focusing on a few select children at first. This highlights both how persuasive she was, to convince the essential children that she needed, but also how highly imaginative she was as well. She was looking at the social hierarchy of the room and acting on how she could win over the trust of the entire classroom through this manner. It is a type of control over her students that becomes more impressive as I think to the difficulty I have with my own kids.

A Cancer has their fair number of weaknesses as well, but unlike many other signs, the weaknesses of a Cancer are somewhat separated from their strengths. Typically a strength taken in the wrong context is the cause of a sign's greatest weakness, but with a Cancer, they have a host of different personality quirks. To start, a Cancer is highly skeptical of strangers, and exhibits this trait to a fault. They are very quick to judge those that they do not know, and will do so typically aiming for a negative impression. This is just how they feel about those that are outside of their immediate social circle and their family – they start from a spot of no trust and must build that trust with a Cancer. A Cancer can also be difficult to talk to unless you know them well. They are fiercely intelligent, but they are not likely to share information with those that they do not know well. They will instead opt to shudder themselves and get to know the other person before they truly reveal themselves.

A Cancer is also highly critical of people that do not share traditional family values. Unlike nearly all other signs, a Cancer's views can take a somewhat political stance. A Cancer is likely to hold deep seeded religious views, and loves the essential idea of a child being raised by their birth mother. They are likely to be anti abortion, and a firm believer in a child being raised by two parents. No matter where you stand on these issues, I believe that getting to know a Cancer really opens up your view on how people can come to stand on these issues. I for one vehemently disagree with many of these points, but after getting to know several Cancers, and thinking aback to my elementary school teacher, I may still disagree but at least I can understand where this viewpoint is coming from. It is not a place of malice or contempt for a different part of society, but rather the strong love that a Cancer has for the children of a family. They believe that the only way to raise these children properly to instill strong values from the mother, and they believe this because it is in their nature to want to do exactly this – they feel they are a necessary person in raising a child, and cannot imagine a home that does not have a loving mother and father that cares deeply for their children.

If you know a Cancer in your life, I suggest that you befriend them as a strong family role model. They exhibit very traditional characteristics of what it means to be a family, and regardless of where you stand on political issues relating to the family, a Cancer can broaden your perspective and help you understand their specific viewpoint. They might appear standoffish at first, and be closeted and unlikely to reveal themselves, but once you get to know them this changes greatly. This is an investment of your time that is certainly worth the effort. You should get to know a cancer and focus on their positive attributes, as they are ideals of the family that are worth sharing.

Chapter 5: Leo

July 23rd – August 22nd

It should be no surprise that Barrack Obama was born on August 4th, making him a Leo. This should come as no surprise because he very much embodies many of the ideals of a Leo: he is confident, persuasive and a natural born leader. If the Aries was driven to success by their desire to win in a competition, it is the Leo that is driven to success for their desire to benefit the group as a whole. A Leo wants nothing more than victory for the people that look up to them. They are given energy, lift and sprit by being in a leadership role. They will strive for such a position, and should they find themselves without it, they can be pessimistic, angry, and feel as though they have no purpose.

It is hard for me to separate a Leo and an Aries. These are two very strong signs; they are dependable, but to get them to rise to action requires certain motivation. For an Aries, this comes in the form of competition and the desire to win. For a Leo, it comes from wanting to do good for people that look up to them. They feel as though they need to be a role model, and need watching eyes on their every action to motivate them; they literally feed off this energy. Being a role model serves two purposes for a Leo – one, it provides the essential energy that they thrive from and gives lift to their sprit. Two, it is a type of check on their own actions. A Leo has a strong moral code, but one that needs to be indebted to another. This is one of the one of the more complex ideas when it comes to astrology, as the strengths of a Leo are dependent on having others view them.

For example, a Leo is only as morally tough as the number of eyes that they have monitoring their actions. In an odd sort of way, a Leo can only be a truly great role model if they have people to look up to them. They see this role as a responsibility and truly do care about those that follow them. This causes a Leo to strive to be responsible. Where they might waver if they were not under the watchful eye of followers, a Leo that is admired can find great moral strength to stand as a representation of what we should all strive for. It is somewhat depressing that when a Leo is not given any sense of authority that their moral backbone is not nearly as strong. If they feel as though they are not a role model, then there is no true moral code you can point to that a Leo will follow. It is a 'dangerous' sign in this way, dependent on their ability to gain the attraction of others so that they themselves have something to motivate themselves.

When a Leo is not in a literal leadership role, they do best when they are being admired. You may see a Leo strive to be an actor, or a public role where they can gain fandom and the appreciation of others. They subsist off of this appreciation, and can become quite bitter when they are not treated with attention. This makes Leo one of the more variable signs in terms of how they may act. When a Leo finds the love of other people around them, they are happy, content and strong. Without it however, they are bitter, highly argumentative, and live without a clear moral code.

If you know a Leo in your life, it can be hard to give them the attention that they seek. It can feel as though you are feeding something awful, but you can't think about it this way. It is not their desire to be liked so much as it is the Leo's *need* to be liked. They did not choose to crave attention, the same way an alcoholic doesn't choose their relationship with alcohol. It is something that they are born with and something that they cannot control. It cannot be overstated that when a Leo is given the love and respect they need, they rise to the occasion and do a wonderful job of spreading that love around. They are not one to take in the love from others and to hold it to themselves. They will opt to share the positive feeling with everyone in the room. They are great philanthropists and want to give back to the community, given they have the opportunity to do so.

It is my suggestion that if you are working with a Leo, that you give them additional responsibilities. If their sign in is any indication, they will rise to the occasion. Just remember this one rule; the more people with eyes on a Leo, the better that Leo will perform. This logic can seem quite counterintuitive to those that are shy, but for a Leo, they truly only feel negative and alone when no one is paying attention to them. With just a little bit of attention, that is when a Leo can truly show off their strengths and have a positive impact on everyone around them.

Chapter 6: Virgo

August 23rd – September 2nd

When I saw sixteen, I got my first job at a small locally owned arts and crafts store. It was a place in town where you could buy paint, canvas, wallpaper, and goods to beautify the home. An elderly couple owned the store. The most surprising thing about the store was that it was open from ten to ten, seven days a week. Mind you, I was one of just three young people working for the store. Most of the time the elderly couple operated that store alone, and even more frequently it was just the husband in the shop. I start with this story because this man represents the Virgo – he is a hard working individual, has great attention to detail and is highly practical.

That arts and crafts store in my town was such a perfect outlet for the owner and his sensibilities that it really shouldn't be any wonder that he worked such long hours. A Virgo is characterized by their extremely strong work ethic, but maybe even more than that, it is in their attention to detail that their personality is at its strongest. When employees like myself would hang up a new item in the store, the owner would come by to make sure that it was done just right. Even if it was a good that would be sitting in the store for just a few hours, he needed to make sure that it was exactly level. Put simply, the man was highly critical of all those around him and their actions. At the time and as a sixteen year old boy, this was the cause of a lot of frustration for myself, but looking back at it now and with the context that he was Virgo, I can now appreciate what the did for that store.

The owner had an attention to detail that was unwavering. If there was a mistake, even in the slightest detail of a product, he needed to fix it. This attention to detail was coupled with extreme practicality, and that made him one of the wisest advisors for home improvements I have ever seen. You could step into that store with an idea for a small home improvement project. Maybe you would know what you would like to accomplish, but you weren't sure about the materials and tools to use. The shop owner could fill in the details that you needed with such clarity, telling you exactly what you needed and how it should be done. He would warn you of the common trouble spots that you would run into, and even give tips for how to rectify the mistakes that you are likely to make along the way. This is the type of attitude of a Virgo, yes they have an eye for attention to detail to the point of it being a fault, but you can see how incredibly useful this was for customers. He was able to answer questions that workers of hardware stores would just scratch their heads at – this was because of his practicality, but also through his work ethic that had put him through so many different home improvement projects that at one point or another he has helped someone with every type of problem. There was no task that you could take to him that was truly unique; because he worked so often that he had seen it all. Furthermore, he understood that no two improvement projects were ever the same. He would listen to the fine details of a customer's request and pick out exactly the types of tools that they needed, specific to not just the task, but that specific job for that specific house.

These are the strengths of the Virgo, but they also are the cause of some of the Virgo's greatest weaknesses. A Virgo cannot stop paying attention to the fine details. This causes great ire in those around the Virgo because the Virgo will point out even the smallest flaws. Have a stain on your shirt, and a Virgo is the first to notice. Complete a project but finish one detail less than optimally, and the Virgo is the first person to point out these flaws. It can be entirely too much to bear for many signs, especially those that are more self-conscious.

The Virgo's strong work ethic is yet another trouble spot. If you have a Virgo in your life, you just have to accept that they need to keep busy and productive for most of their day. There is no such thing as a day off for a Virgo, but more than that, the work that they feel they need to accomplish is often profit driven. Whereas an Aries might have difficulty relaxing on the weekend, deciding instead to do a home improvement project, a Virgo is similar but they would first focus on what would produce profit. A Virgo might decide then to go to the office on the weekend instead of staying home and working on the house. They strive for money because they view it was a way of keeping track of their progress. The more they accumulate, the more that they feel they have done a good job.

It is my suggestion that you try and understand the strong critiques that a Virgo might offer. It can be difficult to listen to what can often just sound like complaints, but remember that a Virgo criticizes because they are perfectionists. Feel assured that they give themselves the same scrutiny that they provide to others – they are not immune to their highly focused critical eye. It is perhaps this critical eye that this is one final detail of a Virgo that bears mention, they do not enjoy the spotlight. I would advise that you do not force a Virgo into any sort of public facing role, as this is something that produces a lot of pressure for a Virgo. Even if they handle the role well, Virgos typically have a strong distaste for public speaking. Focus on the strengths of the Virgo, namely their practicality and work ethic, and mind that their critical eye can be quite difficult to deal with, but the intent of a Virgo is only for improvement.

You are halfway done!

Congratulations on making it to the halfway point of the journey. Many try and give up long before even getting to this point, so you are to be congratulated on this. You have shown that you are serious about getting better every day. I am also serious about improving my life, and helping others get better along the way. To do this I need your feedback. Click on the link below and take a moment to let me know how this book has helped you. If you feel there is something missing or something you would like to see differently, I would love to know about it. I want to ensure that as you and I improve, this book continues to improve as well. Thank you for taking the time to ensure that we are all getting the most from each other.

http://getbook.at/AstrologyBeginner

Chapter 7: Libra

September 23rd – October 22nd

      The Libra is one of the most complicated astrological signs. Libras share the common traits of wanting harmony between all people, but at the same time hate conformity. This seemingly incongruent mentality makes the Libra very difficult to understand as an abstract idea. To truly be able to visualize how the Libra interacts with their environment, you have to have someone specific in mind that was born with this sign. They can often contradict themselves, as is the base nature of their traits, but deep down above all they desire justice for all people no matter how different, and at its base this is the core of their personality. Their experiences help shape how they take this idea out into the world, but you can expect the Libra to be engaged in discussions of equality with others, always promoting the idea of unity but engaging with others that have very different backgrounds to themselves.

      I have known several Libras in my life, and no two of them were ever the same. How they take their approach of harmony to the world is vastly different depending on the individual. I tend to think back to a roommate that I had in college, and how his ideas of the world were shaped over our four years of study. Starting off, my roommate had certain preconceived notions of the world. He believed that power is in the hands of too few, and that is why certain people are born with advantages over others. His ideas on these topics would change greatly over time, but the core principle of a great sharing of the power in the world was central to his being at all times. It is merely in his approach to this idea that changed.

      By the time we graduated, he had spent time in several countries, working on housing and development projects. This was related to his major at the time, but what guided him to these trips, and even his field of study, was that initial desire to put the greater power in the hands of the many that had too little control over their own fate. This exemplifies the Libra and their approach to life; they want to provide the tools to success to all those that they meet. They want everyone to feel inclusive in the group, but to never give up on their own individual personality. They want the world as a whole to reach certain conclusions, but these conclusions need to be inclusive of everyone, not favoring one group over another and allowing for the equal distribution of power for everyone. These are lofty ideals, and you are likely to find the Libra in your own life shares this complex viewpoint.

      It is in the strong moral code of the Libra that the character flaws raise to the surface. A Libra hates the uniformed and the indecisive. When presented with someone that has opportunity but does not seek to take advantage of what they have been given, a Libra would criticize this person and would have immediate ire for their approach to life. For a Libra, they cherish all that they have been given and cannot understand when others do not do the same. They cannot rationalize why others do not examine the world just as they do, even if they come up with different conclusions. The Libra essentially hates ignorance above all else; it is fine to argue with a Libra on a topic and to be well informed, but arguing from an emotional perspective is just simply distasteful for a Libra. They have strong feelings about justice, but they must always back up their beliefs with facts and numbers. This can make Libras difficult to talk to, as for so many of us we have opinions on topics that were formed quickly, and not delved into for detailed analysis. A Libra will confront this aspect of human decision making, which is the reason that many signs naturally do not get along with the Libra.

My suggestion for interacting with Libras is to keep in mind their point of view. They choose to argue with others not to make themselves feel good, not to win a battle, but to disseminate knowledge to others. Truly, they argue for their beliefs because they feel that they are just, and that they must speak for those that do not have a voice. If you can view the Libra from this perspective, their actions not only make more senses as a whole, but you can perhaps truly take away something great from a conversation with a Libra. In addition, a few of the minor traits of a Libra make them great caretakers and fantastic friends. They do not like to be alone, and will always share what they have. These are attributes that I would love to have in anyone that I know. You should make room for a Libra in your life. You must just be aware that their world view can sometimes be such a dominate force in their personality, and that if you can just avoid conflicts stemming from this you will be able to create an amazing bond between yourself and a Libra.

Chapter 8: Scorpio

October 23rd – November 21st

It is helpful for me to tie together the Taurus, Aries and Scorpio. They are three very different signs, but what they have in common in that they are the most forceful and headstrong of the twelve. The Taurus is steady in their actions, the Aries is driven by competition, and the Scorpio is ever striving to find the truth. A Scorpio is naturally competitive, but not to the same degree as an Aries. They are strong willed and do sturdy work, but not to the extent of the Taurus. It is the fact that a Scorpio is unrelenting in their desire for the truth that really shows the strength of the Scorpio's personality. It can be a great asset, but also cause stress in relationships.

Scorpios are smart, brave and doubtful of the word of others. I like to imagine the Scorpio as the skeptic, craving for the truth but being unscrupulous in their sources. They do not treat anything as a truth if it is merely told to them. They need to get to the base information on which others make their assertions. A Scorpio makes for a great journalist, as this drive for the truth not only pushes them towards their goal, but they are also morally flexible and willing to conform to the reality that truth presents. A Scorpio can fall on any side of the political spectrum, and will have their beliefs formed entirely from what they have read and studied. The extent of the material that they have covered will often be massive, making them excellent researchers for academia or news. Unlike other signs that may receive information with preconceived notions, the Scorpio is unique in their ability to clear their mind and view facts separately from the issue at hand.

The benefits of this type of personality are fairly straight forward; they cannot be fooled easily, and they are hyper intelligent. They spend the day wondering about the world about them, but in a grounded and practical sense. They are passionate about the truth, and can be very resourceful about how they obtain information. They can approach arguments and situations from a neutral point of view, making them excellent intermediaries. They can often solve disputes by looking at two sides of an argument, understanding both sides clearly, and then explaining to each side the other's point of view. This might sound unremarkable, but in the moment it is truly something to behold. The fact that a Scorpio can bring people together that have vastly different views is a great strength of their sign. They are also unique in that unlike a Leo which desires to stay in the spotlight, a Scorpio does not crave any sort of fame for their efforts. They merely wish to explain the facts, outline the information as they understand it, and then get out of the way just as quickly as they entered.

There are some natural downsides to this personality type, and these mostly stem from the nature of a Scorpio to get into conflict with most other signs. Unlike the Scorpio, most signs come into a situation with preconceived notions, and are unlikely to be as unrelenting for truth as the Scorpio. This can cause frustration on the part of both parties. In my own experiences, I can think of one coworker that was a Scorpio, and the great arguments that he would cause within the office. I need to mention that as great as he was at solving disputes between two other coworkers, he was just as apt as causing a fight between himself and another. These fights would stem from him making an argument for the opposite of what the rest of the office believed as truth. For example, my Scorpio coworker would argue that the fiscal stimulus package assembled after the 2008 financial crisis was a huge waste of money, and would ultimately benefit no one. For some context, this is an argument that was very much in the moment, and took place around 2009. At the time, the federal government was assembling a large care package for businesses and small governments around the country. The size of this package was roughly eight hundred billion dollars – most in my office had the viewpoint that it was a necessity, and that we would individually benefit from this type of large government package. The Scorpio in the office was easily the most knowledgeable about the stimulus, and was vehemently opposed to it. I'm not going to argue whether or not he was right, because that is aside from the point. The point is that many of us walk into arguments with less than perfect knowledge of what we are discussing. A Scorpio simply doesn't do this, and cannot stand it when others have made up their minds before reading all of the necessary information to truly understand a topic. This caused many small scale fights within the office, and highlights the greatest weakness of a Scorpio; the ability to stir conflict in their desire to know the truth.

If you have a Scorpio in your life, keep them close and try and understand their world view. I give this advice because unlike other signs, their world view is likely to be wholly unique. They have only come to conclusions based on examination and lots of thought and reflection. When they offer solutions to problems, listen to the solution as even if it is not the correct one, it is likely to most well think out. A Scorpio has one last strength that bears mentioning; they are truly great friends. A Scorpio is loyal, but also strives to gain emotional attachment from others in the form of friendship. They love to keep long term friends around them, and value connections that were formed through shared experiences. This is an aspect of the Scorpio's personality that makes them just an overall great person to routinely have in your life. They will always be willing to help you, and they are going to tell you the cold truth about a situation, instead of just glossing it over to stay friendly.

Chapter 9: Sagittarius

November 22nd – December 21st

When I was about twenty three years old, I traveled to Brazil. My field of study was geology and I was researching the rock formations north of Rio de Janeiro. It was here where I met a Sagittarius. She embodied all of the attributes of a Sagittarius, from her great sense of humor, to her idealistic nature, to her ability to say anything no matter how improper. The Sagittarius is a personality built around a sense of humor, and it is their way of looking at the world. A Sagittarius views all events, horrible and beautiful, through this lens of humor. They use it as a way of dealing with negative emotions, and it is rare that you will ever see a Sagittarius in poor spirits. Even when a Sagittarius is depressed, they are likely to be making themselves laugh about their sadness; this is their greatest strength and weakness.

I mentioned that the person that most embodies the Sagittarius I met in Brazil. This is a tender memory for me, as she was one of the most fun loving people that I have ever met. Behind her humor though, her joy for life, sat a different portrait. Deep down she was depressed about her family and prospects in life for her herself and her brothers, but this never showed through to her outward personality. There is no setting I could picture where she could not make even the most saddened person crack a smile. This is the great strength of the Sagittarius, and is such a powerful skill that a Sagittarius is often able to skate through life based on this one attribute. Their humor is more effective on some signs than others, but for the most part once a Sagittarius has started to make you laugh, it puts to the side any tensions that may have been building. They are great at diffusing conflict, both between themselves and another sign, and between two signs fighting with each other.

In addition to their humor, a Sagittarius is creative and artistic. They have a way of expressing an idea through art that few other signs are capable of. The emotion that they display through any medium does not need to be that of humor, although this tends to be what most Sagittarius gravitate towards. This creative and free spirit that they have to expressing their ideas resembles how they like to live their lives. A Sagittarius desires travel and cannot be locked down to one location. They get itchy feet faster than any other sign, and do better when they are frequently moving. It is for this reason that several traveling professionals that I have met have been Sagittarius. Their humor lends itself well to sales, and the ability to travel is an initial allure to any Sagittarius.

The negatives of a Sagittarius essentially come down to their inability to express their emotions other than through art and humor, and their strong desire to never settle down. As a Sagittarius becomes older, their relationships become strained as for many people they cannot continue to travel on a whim. Jobs, family and responsibilities can lock us down and have us feeling like we cannot go anywhere. While this is a common sentiment, it is often too much to bear for a Sagittarius. You have to be careful with this aspect because in real terms it manifests in the Sagittarius being more likely to enact divorce than with other sign. At some point, if they feel like they have no ability to travel, they will want to escape and in the modern world this can mean separation. Please don't take this as overly negative, but just a signal that you need to be aware of the desires of a Sagittarius and that they crave mobility.

My suggestion to you if you have a Sagittarius in your life is to understand how humor plays an essential part of their life. You may find as though a Sagittarius is one dimensional, and only able to treat the world in a childish way through jokes and play, but once you understand that this is the lens in which they view the world, you can start to see deeper into their humor. Their messages about how they view the world and themselves is hidden in their jokes, and if you try to understand their humor more, you will in turn be able to read deeper into their personality.

Chapter 10: Capricorn

December 22nd – January 19th

      The Capricorn is among the most serious of the signs of the zodiac. They are driven, hard working, and have a thirst for knowledge that is only rivaled by the Scorpio. Unlike the Scorpio however, they tend to bend information they receive to fit their world view. Capricorns tend to lean towards believing in more traditional values, praising the home and the responsibility of raising a family. A Capricorn has incredible self control, and much of the conflict that arises with other signs is their inability to understand why other people do not share their same attributes. Capricorns tend to be know-it-alls, and are unforgiving of people that do not value education. This does not always mean that a Capricorn strives for success in academia, but rather they do not understand why others do hold the specific knowledge that they know. A Capricorn can be a difficult sign to interact with, but if you focus on the strengths of responsibility and caring for their family, they feature some unique strengths that can solidify the home.

      My sister is a Capricorn, and shares many of the main attributes of the sign. She is certainly a know-it-all, and this is something that we used to get into conflict about when we were younger. The key to understanding the Capricorn is to grasp that they have difficulty seeing other perspectives. It is then the job of the other signs to try and understand where a Capricorn is coming from. This can be more difficult for some signs than others. What you get in exchange for making this initial handing of the olive branch is a relationship with someone that is determined and caring. A Capricorn is a diligent worker, and one that can apply themselves to any number of fields. There is no telling where you might find a Capricorn working. They could be an artist, a writer, a construction worker or an executive. They do not have any predisposition to preferring one line of work over another; the commonality is that they will handle their job responsibilities to the letter – this is perhaps their greatest strength.

      While a Capricorn may have difficulty understanding the viewpoint of another person, they are quite apt at following instructions. It does not matter the type of work or task that needs to be done, a Capricorn believes that any task can be handled appropriately if you just have the requisite knowledge. They exemplify this idea and live it through and through. You will find that any Capricorn you come across is specifically trained for whatever field they are in. If you discover that a Capricorn is not a working professional, but rather a homemaker, you can expect that they do this to with the backing of any and all resources available to them. They will seek to learn as much as they can about a topic if that topic is related to their work. This promotes their strength at work, but also in their faith to family.

If you have a Capricorn in your life, you may find that you get into quite a few arguments. Have faith that a fight with a Capricorn is not the same as a fight with any other sign. While a Capricorn can certainly be unforgiving, they are also one of the most stubborn signs. The key to working with a Capricorn, regardless of the purpose, is to try and understand their world view. If you can force a Capricorn to let you into their family, they will treat you with great respect and will use their hard work and diligence to your benefit. A Capricorn is a tough sign to interact with, but do not discount their faith to their family and their diligence; these are traits that the world needs.

Chapter 11: Aquarius

January 20th – February 18th

To channel the Aquarius is to become in touch with the protestor within us all; the feeling of rebellion and not settling for anything less than the ideal. This is what the Aquarius represents. They want a better future for man kind, and are willing to fight today to ensure that the world is a better place tomorrow. They can often be highly impractical, and how they interact with others ranges from being very shy to extremely extroverted. The Aquarius is an interesting sign in this way – how they speak with others, the topics that interest them, have little to do with their sign. These instead will be traits that are unique to every Aquarius that you meet. The unifying characteristic of the Aquarius are instead a desire for social justice, and a drive to get out and help those that need it.

In their desire for justice for all people, the Libra and the Aquarius have quite a bit in common. What separates these two personalities is exactly what the Aquarius will do to reach the better tomorrow that they envision. An Aquarius sees a disaster on television and doesn't just want to donate money to solve the problem; they would rather get out there on the ground and help those that need it. I mentioned that their personality type could be shy or extroverted, but these are not a factor in their willingness to help other people. You may know a shy Aquarius for example, and later find out that they volunteer quite frequently. I have a coworker that is an Aquarius, and I discovered this very aspect to her life. I was quite shocked when I discovered just how much of her outside time is dedicated towards helping other people. I had always thought of her as too shy to join a large organization dedicated to helping others, and this was a mistake that I want you to avoid. No matter how closeted or shy an Aquarius may seem, they are always willing to break out of their shell to help other people. It is simply in their nature and they cannot help it. They are perhaps the most charitable of all the signs, almost to a fault. They are idealistic in their view of humanity, and are more likely to be subject to deceit from malicious persons.

The greatest weakness of the Aquarius is there inability to see the world as it really is. They forever hold the view of humanity and the word that man is good, and that we must all do what it takes to help our fellow man, no matter the cost. These are extremely admirable ideals, I can't state that enough, but the cost of these ideals is practicality. An Aquarius looks at the world, the people that are starving that do not have clean water, and they can't help but be unable to understand why this is the case. It is troubling for them that this is the reality that we live in, and they cannot understand the practical causes for why these problems exist. It is this sorrow from the negatives that exist in our world that drive the Aquarius to action. Aside from their positive action to help others however, they surround themselves in sorrow and guilt for what the rest of the world must go through.

An Aquarius not only feels guilty for the people of this earth that do not have the basic necessities, but that they are also unable to open up their feelings about this issue. Only with a Pisces perhaps can an Aquarius truly open up and show their true emotion. Their reaction to being unable to deal with their own emotions is to get out of the home and help other people. They are an interesting sign in this regard; the weakness of the Aquarius on the individual level is a strength for humanity as a whole. Their inability to cope with inequality forces them to action, and the state of the world causes the sorrow that motivates an Aquarius to help others.

If you have an Aquarius in your life, it is my suggestion that you try and be as compassionate as possible. This is a sign that has the weight of the world on their shoulders. It can be difficult to communicate with an Aquarius to try and have them open up and make them feel better. The best you can do is provide them with intellectual conversation and listen to them when they do feel like opening up. As a final note for the Aquarius, they have a strong hatred for broken promises. They often feel let down by the state of the world, and when this is mimicked by individuals that let them down, it causes great frustration. With this in mind, try and keep the promises you keep to an Aquarius – they will greatly appreciate it.

Chapter 12: Pisces

February 19th – March 20th

 The Pisces is the most artistic of all the signs. A Pisces is deeply in touch with his or her own emotions, and is able to have other signs open up to them. You may find that a Pisces expresses themselves through painting, music or writing, but it is almost a certainty that they have some form of creative outlet. A Pisces is happiest when they are with someone close, or when they are by themselves. The Pisces is the most introverted of all the signs, and they enjoy periods of self reflection due to their enjoyment of understanding human emotion. It is this basic drive that creates the strength of the Pisces. Their desire to learn and understand the emotion that they feel and the emotion of others is why they need a creative outlet. They need a way to express the emotion that they feel and to decipherer the emotion of society at large – this is how some of the greatest artistic works in human culture have come to fruition, from this essential drive.

 The greatest strength of the Pisces is their desire to understand themselves and others. They are a necessary sign for other signs to open up to. They understand emotion in a way that no other sign does, and so they can create a feeling of safety and security when other signs cannot. You get the sense that Pisces is a really good listening, and this is true, but they are doing more than just listening to your words. They contextualize the stories of other people and how one's actions affect how they feel. Pisces make excellent social workers and therapists, also well as social science researchers. If they are not helping other people find their true emotions, a Pisces is instead focusing on their own emotion, and trying to bring that to reality through artistic works.

 I have known many Pisces in my life, but the person that I always think of when I try and break down the fundamental of this sign, is a friend from high school that was deeply musical. He was incredible in the way that he would listen to the words of other people. You got the sense that he was doing more than just waiting for his turn to speak, that the was actively thinking not about what to say in response, but just digesting the words of the other person. A Pisces can be so in tune with emotions that it can cause them great pain, as it did for my friend. His creative outlet was music, but I often found that he was depressed. This can be the nature of life for a Pisces, as allowing in the emotion of all those around you can leave a Pisces feeling woeful about life as a whole. The greatest moments for a Pisces are when they are creating something beautiful. It is during these times that their ability to suck in the emotions of others is truly mesmerizing. While they might carry extra baggage for listening to the feelings of others, they are able to invoke these feelings in beautiful art. A Pisces is one of the most creative thinkers in this regard, with an ability to translate emotions to a form in art that any sign can understand. A Pisces is therefore essential for other signs to better understand themselves. They take their talent of understanding emotion and transcribe what is often invisible to us, the common sentiment and emotion of people as a whole.

The greatest weakness of a Pisces is that they are too trusting of others. While a Pisces can see through emotion like no other sign, they cannot see deceit as clearly. A Pisces will miss the forest for the trees when speaking to another person, reading their emotions but not their motivations. Pisces are therefore likely to be caught up in at least one scam or abuse of their trust in their lifetime. Often times this mistrust comes from a romantic relationship, where a Pisces has such faith in their partner that they cannot imagine infidelity. In addition, the Pisces does not like to be criticized, and deals poorly with outside assessment. Remember that they are constantly analyzing their own emotions, and having another person comment about their actions is distasteful to the Pisces for this very reason; they don't need outside analysis because they analyze themselves.

If you have a Pisces in your life, my suggestion to you is to bring them joy however you can. A Sagittarius is a great fit for a Pisces as either a friend or romantic partner. They create positive feelings for a Pisces, making them laugh and find joy in humor. I must also suggest that you be careful with the promises you make to a Pisces. There is a strong chance that broken promises are treated as acts of deceit on the part of this sign, and being truthful whenever possible is going to be greatly preferred. Often it is the revelation that someone close was lying to a Pisces that does more harm than the lie itself. It can be difficult to open up to a Pisces because they do not always reciprocate by opening themselves up. You must remember that their form of expression comes through art, and that you should still utilize their ability to analyze your emotions and help you through situations that are emotionally too much to bear.

Conclusion

Thank you again for downloading *Astrology: A Beginner's Guide to Understanding the 12 Zodiac Signs and Their Secret Meanings.*

There are many resources available for researching the zodiac signs, but I hope that this guide was able to contextualize the emotions, strengths and weaknesses of these different signs in a way that was down to earth and made the topic easier to understand. I stated at the outset of this book that how you decide to use this information is up to you, but I hope that ultimately what this book has allowed you to do is understand the many different perspectives of people. It can be difficult to bond with our fellow man; whether we disagree on politics, lifestyle, or a number of minor differences that separate us. We can sometimes feel that we have nothing in common. It is my sincere hope that this book has shattered that view somewhat, and that you can understand that all people have nothing but the best intentions. It is our perspectives and our inclinations to place certain values above others that give us our differences, but deep down we all want the same loving and caring relationships.

As you go forward, try and use the astrological signs and their characteristics to better understand the people around you. I want you to start with the people that you may have disagreed with in the past on issues. Look at their astrological sign and try to decipher why they hold their certain perspectives. I think that you will find that you have more in common with those that you disagree with than you know, and that in the end, we all cherish and care about our families and each other.

Lastly if you enjoyed this book, it would be much appreciated if you could leave a review on Amazon. The best way for this book to make its way into the hands of more readers is through truthful reviews about this work. Please write what you liked about this book and what could be improved upon. Any and all feedback is helpful as I continue to serve the needs of my readership.

Thank you and good luck!

Help me improve this book

While I have never met you, if you made it through this book I know that you are the kind of person that is wanting to get better and is willing to take on tough feedback to get to that point. You and I are cut from the same cloth in that respect. I am always looking to get better and I wish to not just improve myself, but also this book. If you have positive feedback, please take the time to leave a review. It will help other find this book and it can help change a life in the same way that it changed yours. If you have constructive feedback, please also leave a review. It will help me better understand what you, the reader, need to make significant improvements in your life. I will take your feedback and use it to improve this book so that it can become more powerful and beneficial to all those who encounter it.

http://getbook.at/AstrologyBeginner

REMEMBER TO JOIN THE GROUP NOW!

If you have not joined the Mastermind Self Development group yet, now is your time! You will receive videos and articles from top authorities in self-development as well as a special group only offers on new books and training programs. There will also be a monthly member only draw that gives you a chance to win any book from your Kindle wish list!

If you sign up through this link http://www.mastermindselfdevelopment.com/specialreport you will also get a special free report on the Wheel of Life. This report will give you a visual look at your current life and then take you through a series of exercises that will help you plan what your perfect life looks like. The workbook does not end there; we then take you through a process to help you plan how to achieve that perfect life. The process is very powerful and has the potential to change your life forever. Join the group now and start to change your life!
http://www.mastermindselfdevelopment.com/specialreport

MASTERMIND
Self Development

You will also love these other great titles from Mastermind Self Development!

You will want to check out these other great titles Mastermind Self Development. All available in the Kindle store or you can just click on covers below.

http://mybook.to/positivethink

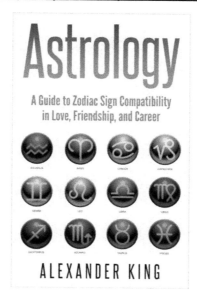

http://getbook.at/Astrologyguide

You can also find these titles by searching them in the Kindle store on Amazon.

Lightning Source UK Ltd.
Milton Keynes UK
UKHW032052070121
376637UK00005B/116